WHAT'S INSIDE?
SUBMARINES

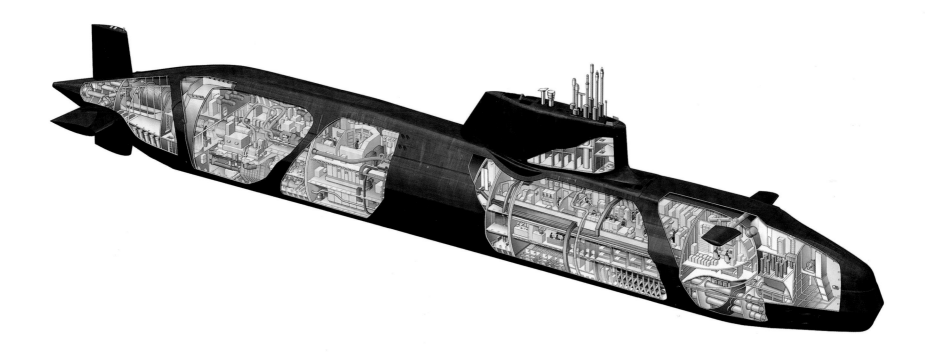

WHAT'S INSIDE?
SUBMARINES

Sandy Creek
NEW YORK

An Imprint of Sterling Publishing
387 Park Avenue South
New York, NY 10016

Editorial and design by
Amber Books Ltd
74–77 White Lion Street
London N1 9PF
United Kingdom

Series Editor: Michael Spilling
Design: Brian Rust and Andrew Easton
Picture Research: Terry Forshaw

ISBN 978-1-4351-5371-4

Manufactured in China
Lot #:
2 4 6 8 10 9 7 5 3 1
09/12

Picture Credits
Photographs
BAE Systems: 3, 42, 43, 44; Cody Images: 6, 8, 10, 11, 12, 18, 19, 20;
Mary Evans Picture Library: 7 (Suddeutsche Zeitung)
Getty Images: 34 (Hulton/Oleg Nikishin), 35 (AFP), 36 (Laski Diffusion)
Mike Greaves: 30; NL Defence Audio Visual Services: 31, 32
U.S. Department of Defense: 14, 15, 16, 22, 23, 24, 26, 27, 28, 38, 39, 40
Artworks
Amber Books/Tony Gibbons: 21, 37; Art-Tech/Aerospace: 25, 29;
Art-Tech/De Agostini: 9, 13, 17, 33; BAE Systems: 1, 45; John Batchelor: 41

Contents

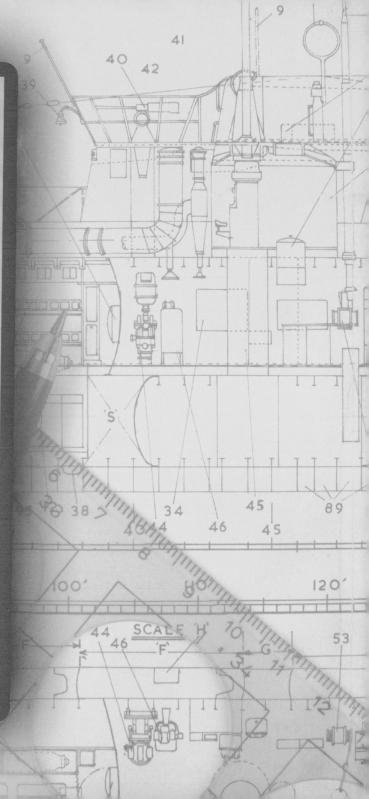

U-9 (1910)

In 1910, Europe's military powers prepared for war. The German Navy built *U-9* in 1910, followed by four similar submarines in 1910 and 1911. When World War I (1914–1918) began, *U-9* went into action.

During the war, Germany built 375 **submarines**, termed **U-boats**, to attack the **merchant shipping** of Britain, France, Russia, and the United States.

Submarine Warfare

Submarines were new war machines. Before 1914 they had been used only a few times—and without much success. At first, naval commanders on both sides believed submarines could not defeat surface warships

U-boat officers drink a toast to celebrate the sinking of an enemy merchant ship.

in battle. Subs were expected to sink only merchant ships carrying enemy supplies. Then, just after the war began, *U-9* **torpedoed** and sank three British warships in just a single hour. This surprise victory proved for the first time that submarines could become powerful naval weapons.

A Short, but Deadly Career

U-9 was 188 feet (57 m) long and had a crew of four officers and 25 men. Her two **kerosene engines** were for surface sailing and her two electric motors were for

Did you know?

• U-Boot is the German term for any type of submarine. U-Boot is short for *Unterseeboot* ("under-sea boat"). In English, only German Navy submarines are called U-boats.

• A submarine has two top speeds: surface and underwater. Speeds of vessels are measured in knots (kt), with 1 knot equaling 1.15 miles per hour (1.85 km/h).

underwater operations. *U-9* traveled on the surface at a speed of 14 **knots**—or 16 miles per hour (26 km/h). Underwater, she moved at a speed of 8 knots—or 9 miles per hour (14.5 km/h). Armed with four **torpedo** tubes and a cannon, *U-9* sank four warships and 14 merchant ships in two years of military service, before being retired in 1916.

The crew of *U-9* stands at attention on deck while stationed on the Baltic Sea.

Conning tower

Periscope

Torpedoes

Propeller

Sleeping compartments

Engines

Type XXI U-Boat (1944)

World War II started in 1939, and this time the warring navies knew how important submarines would be. Germany's latest U-boats were faster and more deadly than ever.

● ● ● ● ● ● ● ● ● ● ● ● ●

World War II (1939–1945) subs had improved underwater capabilities. Germany's XXI Type U-boats were designed to go deeper and stay **submerged** longer than any other submarine.

The "Electric Boat"

The main navies of the **Allies** competed with the **Axis** sea powers to produce submarines. Sub design saw great advances in torpedoes, range of travel, and in batteries for the electric motors. Germany's great hope was the Type

These Type XXI U-boats under construction were captured by the Allies.

The Type XXI's powerful engines and electric motors combined with a sleek hull for speed above and below the water.

XXI, first **launched** in 1943. These were termed "electric boats" because they could operate underwater for three days without needing to surface and recharge batteries.

The U-boat that Never Fought

On the surface, the Type XXI was fast, moving at a top speed of 15 knots—or 18 miles per hour (29 km/h). Submerged, the sub was even faster at 17 knots—19 miles per hour (32 km/h). The Type XXI was 251 feet long (76 m), had six torpedo tubes, and a crew of five officers and 52 men. She could load and fire torpedoes at a rate

of almost one a minute, six times faster than earlier U-boats. Although 118 Type XXI subs were built, only two ever saw action. Allied airpower kept these subs in port and also destroyed docks and navy yards. If Type XXI U-boats had been launched in force two years earlier, Germany might have won the war at sea.

Did you know?

• More than half the U-boats lost during the war were sunk by aircraft.

• France's Bay of Biscay was known as the "Valley of Death" because Allied planes sank 66 U-boats there.

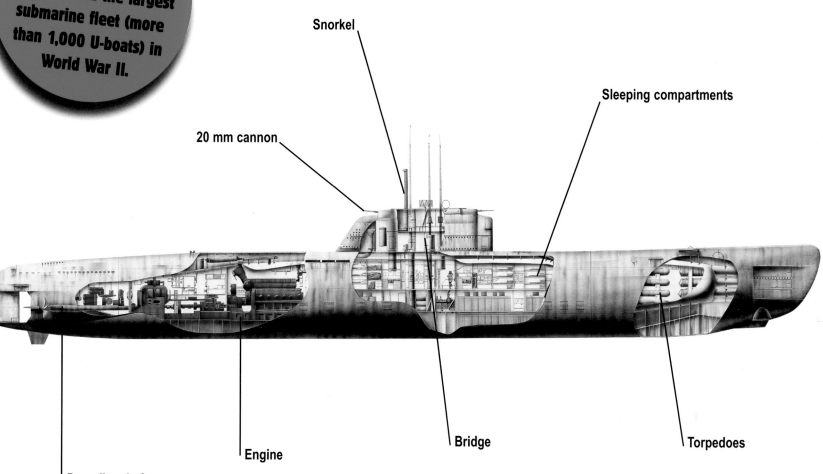

FACT
Germany had the largest submarine fleet (more than 1,000 U-boats) in World War II.

Snorkel

Sleeping compartments

20 mm cannon

Bridge

Torpedoes

Engine

Propeller shaft

USS *Nautilus* (1954)

The U.S. Navy's fleet entered the Nuclear Age in 1954 when USS *Nautilus* launched as the world's first nuclear-powered submarine. The Soviet Union's first nuclear-powered sub appeared in 1958.

Eventually, **nuclear-powered** submarines were armed with **guided missiles** carrying **nuclear warheads**. The **Cold War** between the West and the Soviet-led countries entered an even more dangerous phase.

Journey to the North Pole

Nautilus could stay underwater as long as necessary because nuclear-powered subs need not surface and recharge batteries. She was 320 feet (98 m) long and operated at a high speed of 23 knots—or 26 miles per hour (43 km/h). She had a crew of 13 officers and 92 men, and was armed with six torpedo tubes. In 1958, *Nautilus* traveled for two weeks under the polar ice

A tug accompanies *Nautilus* through the Panama Canal.

to become the first watercraft to reach the North Pole.

From Missions to Museum

Nuclear power made long underwater missions possible, and no one knew where a nuclear sub would appear next. The Soviets' own nuclear subs also often surfaced in

Harbor tugs steer USS *Nautilus* across California's San Francisco Bay, taking her to a dock at Naval Station Treasure Island.

unexpected places in the world. Newer subs carried missiles with nuclear warheads, so it seemed no country could prevent an attack in a nuclear war. By the early 1960s, the U.S. Navy had 26 nuclear submarines, with 30 more being built. In 1980 *Nautilus* was **decommissioned** and **refitted** to prepare her to be part of a museum dedicated to submarine history.

Did you know?

- In her 25-year career, *Nautilus* traveled almost 500,000 miles (800,000 km) across the oceans and seas of the world.

- In 1985 the decommissioned *Nautilus* was towed from a shipyard in Vallejo, California, to Groton, Connecticut, to become part of the Submarine Force Museum.

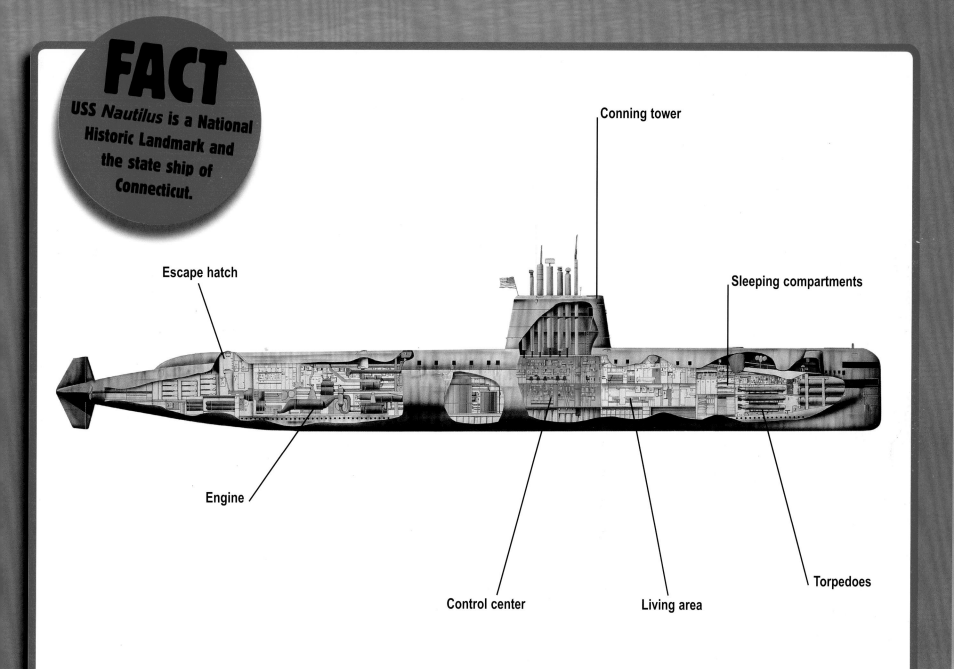

FACT

USS Nautilus is a National Historic Landmark and the state ship of Connecticut.

Conning tower

Escape hatch

Sleeping compartments

Engine

Control center

Living area

Torpedoes

HMS Resolution (1966)

Britain's HMS *Resolution* was among the first submarines armed with missiles fitted with nuclear warheads. Nuclear-armed subs were the next phase in the Cold War between NATO and the Warsaw Pact countries of Eastern Europe.

By the 1960s, Cold War air and missile defenses were about even. When nuclear-powered and armed subs began roaming the seas, no country could be sure its defenses were secure enough.

Missiles Like Spears

In the naval tradition, *Resolution* gave its name to a whole **class** of nuclear-powered **boats** (*Resolution* Class) in the Royal Navy Submarine Service. These subs were armed with ballistic missiles, meaning missiles that are not guided in flight. Instead, after being fired they fly like a spear toward their targets. These missiles usually had several warheads that are timed to explode as they approach the ground.

Resolution makes her way along a Scottish shoreline.

Submarine Launch Platform

A *Resolution* Class submarine's speed was 20 knots—or 22 miles per hour (37 km/h)—surfaced. Submerged, the sub traveled at 25 knots—or 28 miles per hour (46 km/h). Because the boat never had to stop, it needed two full crews, totaling 143

Did you know?

• Most watercraft are described according to size, from boats to ships (small to large), but submarines are all termed "boats," no matter how large they are.

• The first British nuclear submarines were named after Royal Navy battleships of the past: *Resolution*, *Repulse*, *Renown*, and *Revenge*. This showed that submarines (although called "boats") were considered as important as large battleships.

officers and men. These subs were 425 feet (129.5 m) in length and carried 16 Polaris nuclear-armed missiles. *Resolution* Class subs comprised Britain's main nuclear missile **launch platform** for 30 years, until they were replaced in 1994 by a new class of submarines.

The Royal Navy nuclear-powered submarine *Resolution* is serviced while tied up at a British dock.

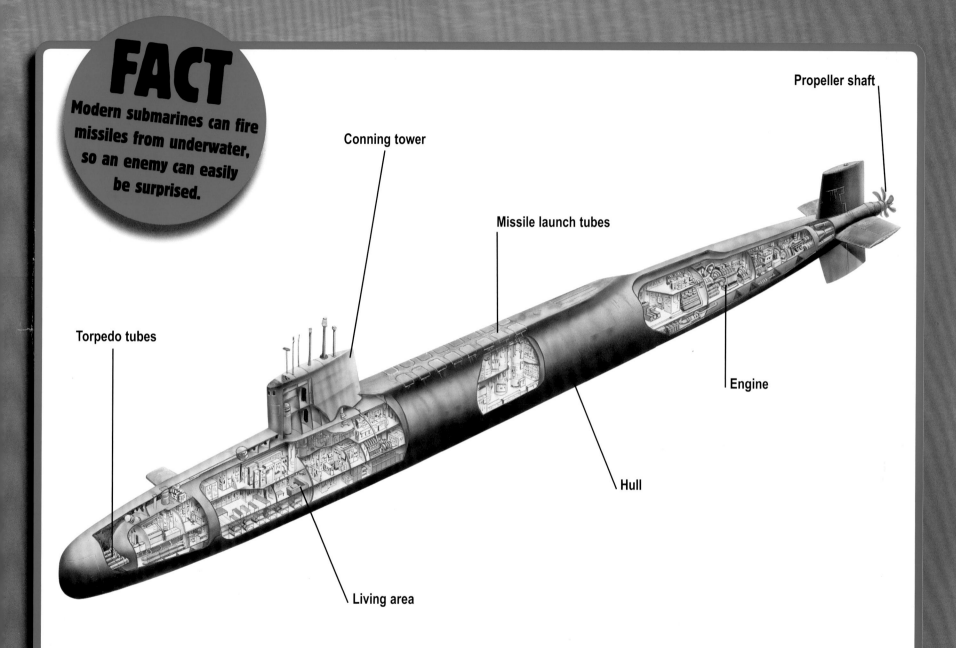

FACT

Modern submarines can fire missiles from underwater, so an enemy can easily be surprised.

Propeller shaft

Conning tower

Missile launch tubes

Torpedo tubes

Engine

Hull

Living area

USS Los Angeles (1974)

USS *Los Angeles* leads a class of nuclear-powered submarines armed with missiles and equipped with the most advanced electronics. They can patrol in deep waters where they are not detected.

Los Angeles Class subs would strike back if an enemy launched missiles at the United States. Because they are difficult to attack, these subs are a **nuclear deterrent** to starting a war.

Fast and Heavily Armed

First built in 1972, *Los Angeles* Class "fast-attack" subs are the heart of the U.S. Navy's submarine force. They are 362 feet (110 m) in length and have 129 crew members. They are armed with four torpedo tubes and with Tomahawk land-attack and Harpoon anti-ship missiles. Their surface speed is 20 knots—or 23 miles per hour (37 km/h). Submerged, their top speed is 33 knots—38 miles per hour (61 km/h).

Los Angeles **is tied up at its home port, Pearl Harbor, Hawaii.**

Officers and crew of *Los Angeles* take their positions on deck and on the sail's conning tower as they enter Apra Harbor, Guam.

runs the submarine. This "burning" is a **nuclear fission** process that occurs in the reactor. Of 62 subs built in this class, 41 were still in service in 2013, with 21 retired.

Refuel Once in 30 Years

The *Los Angeles* sail (the structure on top of the vessel) is specially designed for penetrating thick ice. This sub can operate at 650 feet (200 m) beneath the surface. Powered by a **nuclear reactor**, *Los Angeles* can stay submerged for many weeks and does not need to be "refueled" for 30 years. **Nuclear fuel** is material such as uranium-235, which "burns" to produce the energy that

Did You Know?

• Adding the word "the" to a ship's name is incorrect. Instead of saying, "Yesterday, the *Los Angeles* arrived in port," it should be: "Yesterday, *Los Angeles* arrived in port."

• "USS" before an American naval vessel's name stands for "United States ship." The British "HMS" means "Her (or His) Majesty's ship."

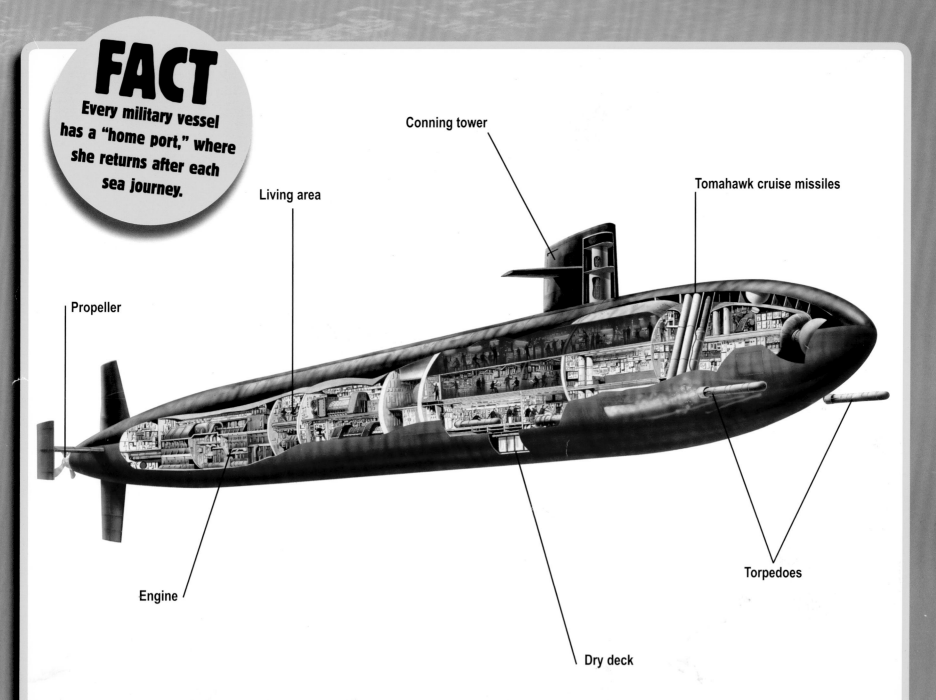

FACT
Every military vessel has a "home port," where she returns after each sea journey.

Conning tower

Tomahawk cruise missiles

Living area

Propeller

Engine

Dry deck

Torpedoes

USS Ohio (1979)

Nuclear-powered submarines became ever more powerful in the 1980s. Each side in the Cold War wanted to convince the other that nuclear war would be a disaster for everyone.

In 1979, the U.S. Navy launched USS *Ohio*, armed with long-range missiles. Few Soviet cities or military bases would be out of range of *Ohio's* weaponry.

Tomahawks and Tridents

Each *Ohio* Class nuclear-powered submarine is armed with many long-range missiles. There are 22 firing tubes, each with seven Tomahawk cruise missiles, totaling 154 missiles. The boat's 14 Trident missiles can reach targets 4,600 miles (7,400 km) to 7,500 miles (12,000 km) distance. For action against warships, there are four torpedo tubes, centrally

In dry dock, USS *Ohio* has her weaponry changed from ballistic to guided missiles.

positioned **midships**. The *Ohio* Class submarine fleet carries out underwater patrols all around the world.

Long Patrols, Deep Dives

Ohio Class submarines can operate at a depth of more than 800 feet (240 m). Their patrols usually last about 70 days. In 2010, USS *Maine*

Stopped off the coast of Puget Sound, Washington State, *Ohio* prepares to transfer news media visitors to another vessel that lies alongside.

Did you know?

• All the *Ohio* Class submarines, except for the USS *Henry M. Jackson*, are named for U.S. states.

• The U.S. Navy has 18 *Ohio* Class nuclear submarines.

conducted the sub fleet's longest-ever patrol—105 days. The 15 officers and 140 enlisted men are divided into two complete crews to keep the sub going night and day. These subs are large, at 560 feet (170 m) in length. They can sail at 12 knots (14 mph; 22 km/h) surfaced, and make up to 25 knots (29 mph; 46 km/h) submerged.

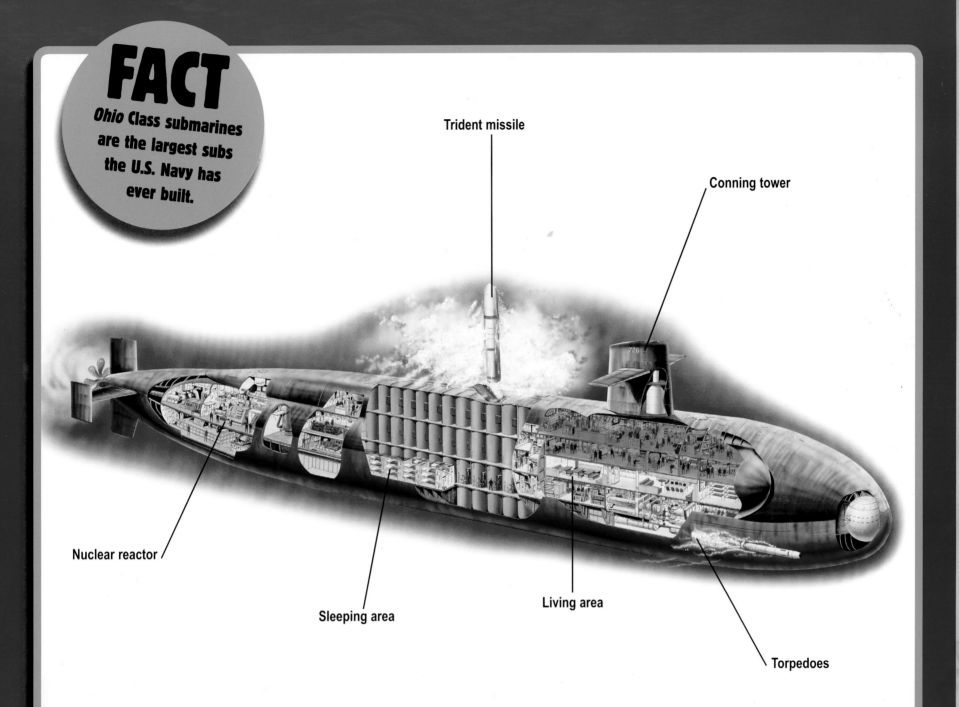

FACT

Ohio Class submarines are the largest subs the U.S. Navy has ever built.

Trident missile

Conning tower

Nuclear reactor

Sleeping area

Living area

Torpedoes

HNLMS Zeeleeuw (1987)

Zeeleeuw ("Sea Lion") is a Royal Netherlands Navy submarine built in 1987. She was designed after *Walrus*, which gave her name to a class of subs. These small, specialized submarines operated secretly around the world, gathering information.

● ● ● ● ● ● ● ● ● ● ● ● ● ● ● ●

Walrus Class submarines were important to **NATO** during the Cold War because they had the latest technology to listen in on the enemy's communications. Still in service, *Zeeleeuw* runs silently and has a highly-trained crew.

A Blue-Water Boat

During the Cold War most U.S. submarines were either brown-water (coastal) subs or large, nuclear-powered blue-water (ocean-going) boats. *Walrus* Class subs were

Like a wandering whale, *Zeeleeuw* moves through waters off Scotland.

31

With her sail dark against the sunlit shore, *Zeeleeuw* flies the Dutch flag from her conning tower.

bases and their vessels. *Zeeleeuw* is 223 feet (68 m) long and has a speed of 13 knots—or 15 miles per hour (24 km/h) when traveling on the surface. Her underwater speed is 20 knots—or 23 miles per hour (37 km/h). She has four torpedo tubes and carries antisubmarine weaponry.

unusual because they were blue-water boats with diesel engines and electric motors.

Gathering Intelligence

Walrus Class subs are used in "near-shore" intelligence-gathering operations. They have roamed silently underwater along the coasts of the Adriatic, Africa, the Caribbean, and Iraq. In 2010, a *Walrus* sub helped combat Somali pirates. The boat submerged to go close to shore, undiscovered, and listened to radio communications between pirate land

Did you know?

• A "green-water navy" is a defense force with limited operations close to land.

• A "brown-water navy" operates along coastlines, where river mouths make the water brown from silt carried from inland.

• A "blue-water navy" is a naval force capable of operating across the deep oceans of the world.

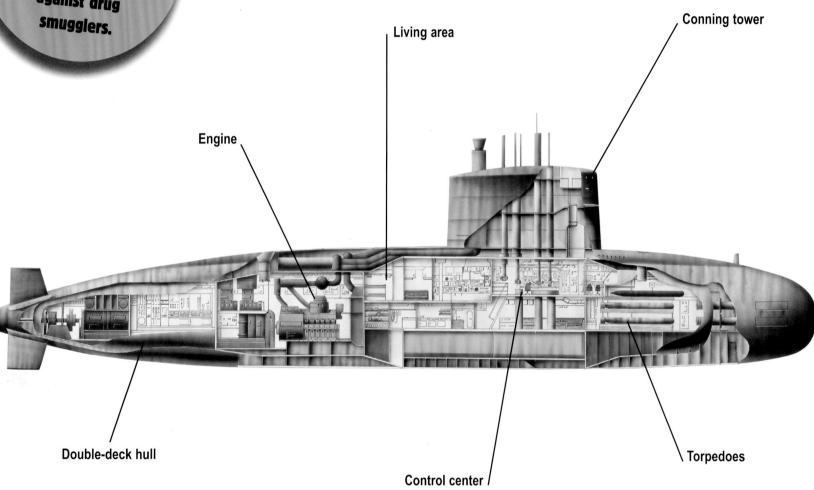

FACT
In 2002, *Zeeleeuw* served in the Caribbean against drug smugglers.

Living area

Conning tower

Engine

Double-deck hull

Control center

Torpedoes

RFS Kursk (1994)

Kursk was a Russian nuclear-powered cruise missile-armed submarine, one of the first vessels completed after the fall of the Soviet Union. She was lost with her entire crew in August 2000.

Kursk was an "Oscar II" Class submarine serving with Russia's Northern Fleet in the Barents Sea. An accidental explosion caused by a fire in the torpedo room sent her to the bottom of the sea.

Pride of the Fleet

At 505 feet (154 m) in length, *Kursk* was one of the largest attack submarines in the world. She was the pride of the Northern Fleet and had just finished a successful mission tracking the U.S. Sixth Fleet in the Mediterranean. Her speed was 16 knots (18 mph; 30 km/h) surfaced and 32 knots (37 mph; 59 km/h) submerged. She could operate at a depth of 1,600 feet (500 m).

This aerial view shows *Kursk*'s unusual, streamlined sail.

Did you know?

• When sunken ships are salvaged, technicians often cut them into pieces underwater, using special tools.

• In salvage operations, such as the raising of *Kursk*, workers must be careful not to make sparks. These can set off dangerous gases.

Loss of All Hands

Most of *Kursk's* 112-man crew men died in the explosion. A second and larger explosion—caused by a fire setting off torpedo warheads—occurred within minutes. *Kursk* sank to a depth of 330 feet (100 m). At the time of the sinking, she carried 28 long-range missiles. The resulting salvage operation was always under threat of a disastrous explosion. Fortunately, none of the warheads was nuclear, which would have endangered the Russian city of Severmorsk and its naval base, 84 miles (135 km) away.

Pictured in summertime, *Kursk* is docked at her home port in northern Russia, Zapadnaya Lista.

FACT
At least seven songs and two stage plays have been produced about the loss of *Kursk*.

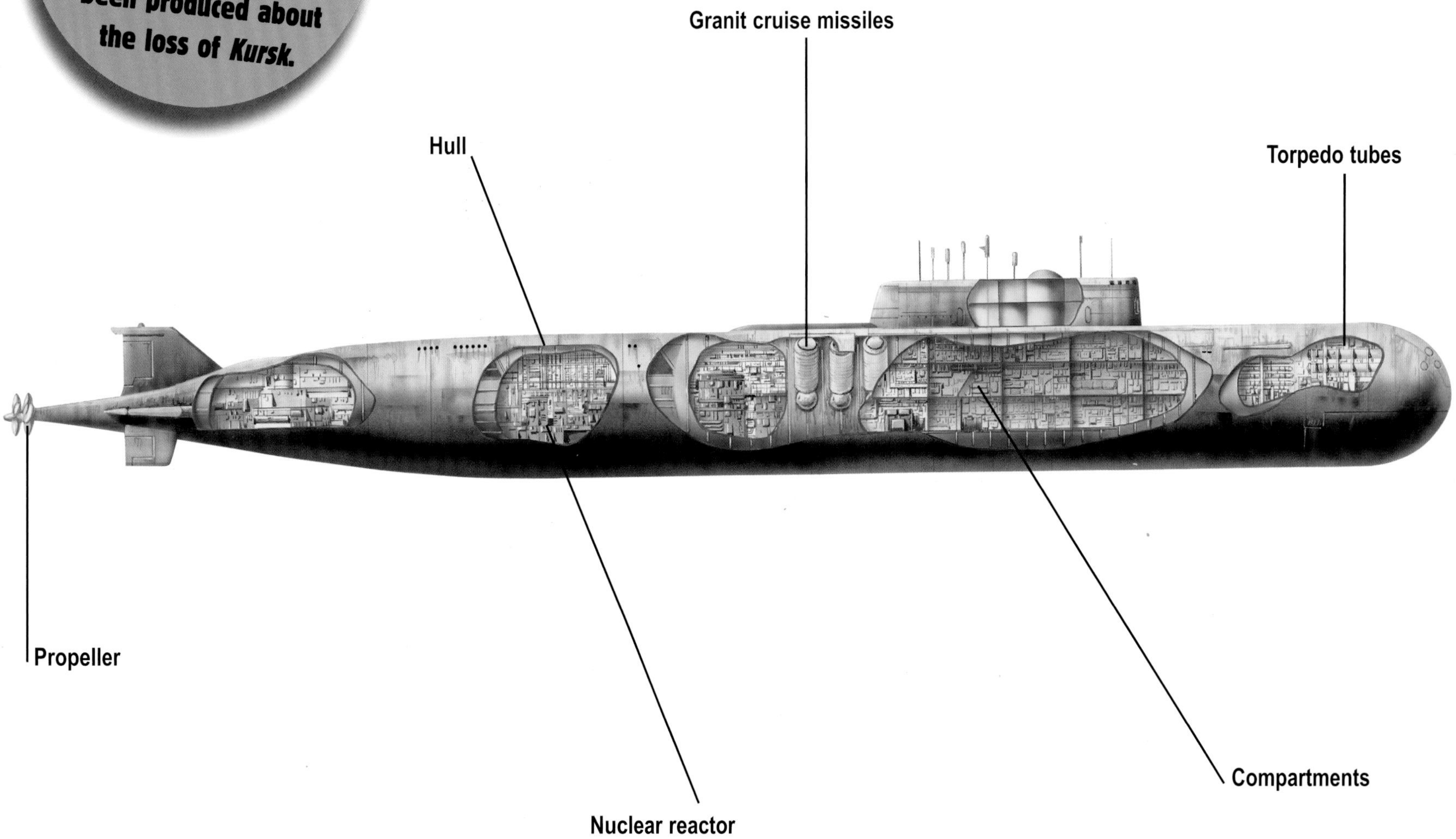

Granit cruise missiles

Hull

Torpedo tubes

Propeller

Nuclear reactor

Compartments

USS Seawolf (1995)

Following the end of the Cold War, the U.S. Navy wanted submarines that were faster, better armed, and able to operate deeper than any Soviet sub. *Seawolf* was to be such a submarine.

Seawolf was supposed to be the first of 29 boats in her class. When the Cold War ended, however, plans to build these subs fell apart.

Faster, Deeper, Quieter

Seawolf was launched in 1995 by the Electric Boat Division of General Dynamics at Groton, Connecticut. *Seawolf* Class subs were intended to replace the *Los Angeles* Class in the submarine fleet. They had more speed and could go deeper and run more silently than *Los Angeles* Class subs. When the Soviet Union collapsed in 1991, the *Seawolf* Class seemed unnecessary, and much too expensive. Only three of the planned 29 were built.

In 2007, *Seawolf* was stationed in New London, Connecticut.

New Missions for Subs

Seawolf was designed to patrol worldwide, but the end of the Cold War reduced blue-water operations. The need now was for coastal-waters missions—operations against terrorism and piracy. *Seawolf* is 353 feet (108 m) long. She can make more than 18 knots (21 mph; 34 km/h)

Did you know?

• The Electric Boat Division of General Dynamics has been the main builder of U.S. Navy submarines for more than 100 years.

• In 1899, the company was established in Groton, Connecticut, to build submersibles designed by inventor John P. Holland. In 1900, Electric Boat built USS *Holland*, the first submarine ever commissioned in the U.S. Navy.

surfaced and 25 knots (29 mph; 47 km/h) submerged. Crewed by 15 officers and 101 men, *Seawolf* can operate at depths greater than 800 feet (240 m). She is armed with eight torpedo tubes as well as land-attack and anti-ship missiles.

Atlantic waves surge over *Seawolf* in 1997. She is undergoing tests—or sea trials—to examine her seaworthiness and mechanical readiness.

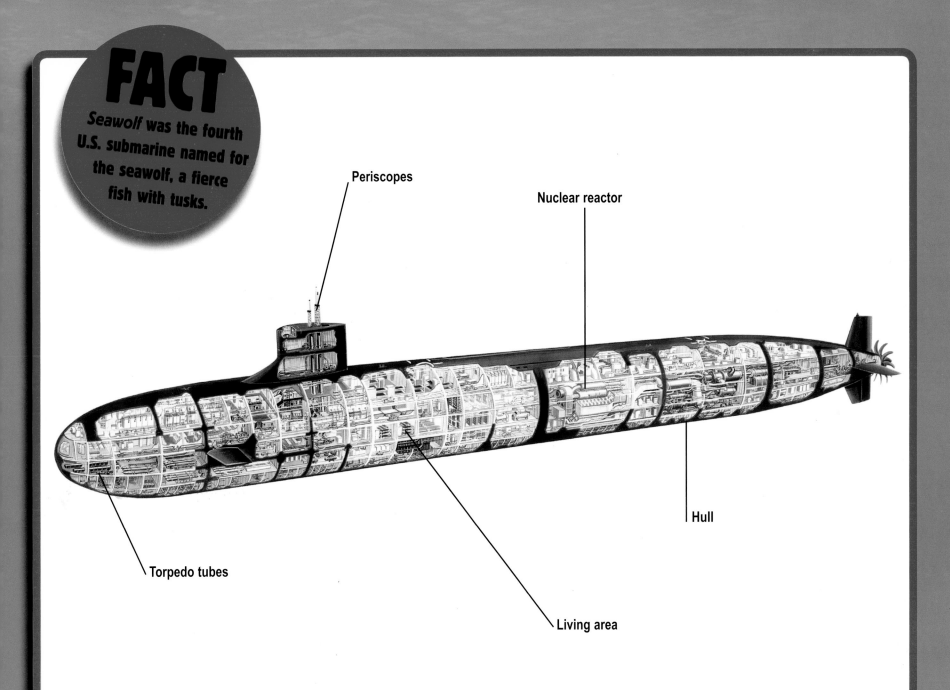

FACT

Seawolf was the fourth U.S. submarine named for the seawolf, a fierce fish with tusks.

Periscopes

Nuclear reactor

Hull

Torpedo tubes

Living area

HMS Astute (2007)

In 1997, British shipbuilders began work on HMS *Astute*, designed to be among the world's fastest and best-equipped nuclear subs. More than 10,000 excited spectators attended her launching in 2007.

The sub was fully operational by 2010, and *Astute* was **commissioned** into the Royal Navy. Unfortunately, she had many mechanical and design problems that needed years to solve.

Hunter-Killer Subs

The planned seven submarines of the *Astute* Class were "hunter-killer" boats designed to attack enemy submarines. They also had to protect aircraft carriers at sea. To keep up with the fast carriers, *Astute* needed a top speed of 30 knots (35 mph; 54 km/h). She had technical troubles from the start, however. Although impressive in length at 318 feet (97 m), *Astute* was not fast enough.

Astute sits, under construction, in dry dock.

During 2010 sea trials, *Astute* sails in the waters of Scotland's River Clyde, along with the Royal Navy's new guided missile destroyer, HMS *Dauntless*.

computer difficulties, and questionable quality of some parts. By 2013, *Astute* could dive to 984 feet (300 m), but was still undergoing further improvements.

Fixing Astute's Problems

During sea trials in 2010, *Astute* ran aground and had to be towed back to base. Next time out, her power plant had problems, and she was towed home again. Tests of her weaponry were successful—these included Tomahawk land-attack missiles and anti-submarine torpedoes. She has six torpedo tubes. The crew numbers 98 officers and enlisted men. Work continued in order to solve *Astute's* problems—flooding, metal corrosion,

Did you know?

• The main task of modern submarines is anti-submarine warfare: they are designed to find and fight each other in the depths of the ocean.

• Of the seven *Astute* Class submarines planned in 1997, only two were completed (*Astute* and *Ambush*). Both were still undergoing trials fifteen years later.

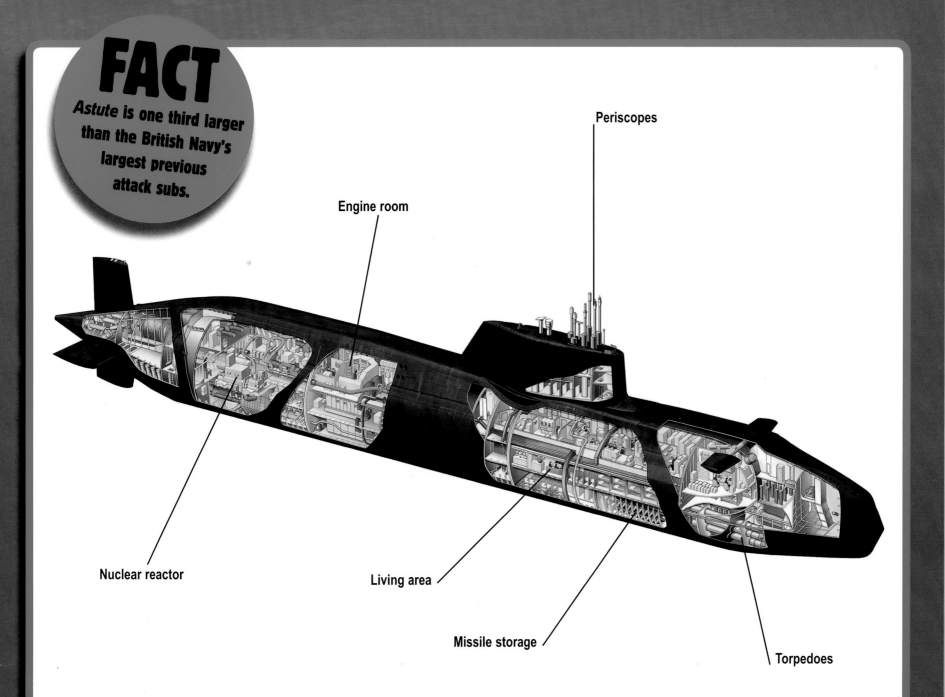

FACT

Astute is one third larger than the British Navy's largest previous attack subs.

Periscopes

Engine room

Nuclear reactor

Living area

Missile storage

Torpedoes

Glossary

Allies (The)—Nations on the same side against Germany and her supporting nations in World Wars I and II

Axis (The)—Germany and the nations who fought on her side in World War II

boat—term often used for a submarine

class (of vessels)—a type or design of similar vessels, usually named after the first one launched

Cold War—state of hostility between U.S.-led countries and Soviet-led countries from 1945 to 1990

commission—to officially enter a vessel into a navy

conning tower—the structure on a submarine where officers can keep watch when surfaced

decommission—to officially remove a vessel from a navy

guided missiles—missiles that are controlled in flight

kerosene engines—engines fueled by kerosene

knot—measurement of a vessel's speed per hour

launch—to put a boat being built into the water for the first time

launch platform—equipment, bases, aircraft, or vessels used for launching missiles

merchant shipping/ships—civilian vessels for carrying cargo across the seas

midships—in the middle of a ship

NATO—North Atlantic Treaty Organization; a military alliance led by the United States

nuclear deterrent—weapons meant to stop (deter) a nuclear conflict

nuclear fuel—material used to produce nuclear energy

nuclear fission—a process in which atoms are made to release energy

nuclear-powered—equipment that uses nuclear energy for movement or electricity

nuclear reactor—equipment that controls nuclear fission to produce energy for power

nuclear warhead—a missile's tip that contains nuclear explosives

refit/refitted—repair and replace vessel's equipment and machinery

submarine/sub—a vessel that can operate underwater

submerge—to go underwater

submersible—something which can be submerged or operates while submerged

torpedo—a self-propelled missile fired from a torpedo tube and which travels underwater

torpedoed—to attack with or be attacked by a torpedo

U-boat—a German navy submarine

Warsaw Pact—an alliance formed between the Soviet Union and the countries of Eastern Europe

Index